QUESTION 1

Which three statements are true about Master-Detail relationships? (Choose three.)

A. Standard objects can be on the detail side of a custom object in a Master-Detail relationship.
B. Master-Detail relationships cannot be converted to a look-up relationship.
C. Deleting a master record in a Master-Detail relationship deletes all related detail records.

D. Master-Detail relationships can convert to a lookup relationship if no roll-up summary fields exist on the master object.
E. A Master-Detail relationship cannot be created if the custom object on the detail side already contains data.

Correct Answer: CDE

QUESTION 2

In order to delete Opportunities, Universal Containers would like sales reps

to submit requests for approval from their sales manager. What can be

used to meet these requirements?

A. Approval Process with Time-Dependent Workflow action.
B. Approval Process with Apex Trigger.
C. Two-step Approval Process.
D. Process Builder with Submit for Approval Action.

Correct Answer: C

QUESTION 3

An app builder at Universal Containers would like to prevent users from

creating new records on an Account related list by overriding standard

buttons. Which two should the app builder consider before overriding standard buttons? (Choose two.)

A. Standard buttons that are not available for overrides can still be hidden on page layouts.
B. Standard buttons can be changed on lookup dialogs, list views, and search result layouts.
C. Standard buttons can be overridden, relocated on the detail page, and relabeled.
D. Standard buttons can be overridden with a Visualforce page.

Correct Answer: BD

QUESTION 4
Which three Salesforce functionalities are ignored when processing field updates in workflow rules and approval processes? (Choose three.)

A. Field-level security
B. Record type picklist value assignments
C. Multiple currencies
D. Validation rules
E. Decimal places and character limits

Correct Answer: BCE

QUESTION 5
An app builder has been asked to integrate Salesforce with an external web service. The web service must be notified every time an Opportunity is Won.

Which two can satisfy this requirement? (Choose two.)

A. Use a workflow rule and an outbound message.

B. Write a trigger to use Apex Managed Sharing to grant access with the Process Improvement team.

C. Use a process and an outbound message.

D. Use a process and Apex code.

Correct Answer: AD

QUESTION 6
Which two ways can an app builder grant object-level access to users? (Choose two.)

A. Public Groups
B. Permission Sets
C. Roles
D. Profiles

Correct Answer: BD

QUESTION 7
Universal Containers' CEO has asked that all deals with more than a 40% discount get automatically sent to the VP of Finance. He will review these details without the sales rep needing to take action.

Which two ways can this be accomplished without building code? (Choose two.)

A. Create a new approval process that has automatic submission enabled in the entry criteria.
B. Launch a flow that uses the submit for approval action to submit deals for approval.
C. Launch a new approval process that has automatic submission enabled as an initial submission action.
D. Create a new process with a submit for approval action to automatically submit deals for approval.

Correct Answer: BD

QUESTION 8
What feature can an app builder use to automatically assign cases that have been open longer than three days to the next support tier?

A. Case Assignment Rules

B. Case Escalation Rules

C. Case Business Rules

D. Case Auto Response Rules

Correct Answer: B

QUESTION 9

A custom field on an account is used to track finance information about a customer. Only members of the Finance Team have access to this field. However, the business wants to allow one customer service agent, who is assigned the customer service profile, read-only access to this field for special circumstances.

What is the recommended solution to grant the customer service agent access to the field?

A. Update the Customer Service Profile already assigned to the agent to allow for read-only access to the field via Field Level Security.

B. Create a permission set that allows read-only access to the field via Field Level Security and assign it to the agent.

C. Create a new profile to allow for read-only access to the field via Field Level Security and assign it to the agent.

D. Update the custom field's Field Level Security in setup to allow the agent read-only access to the field.

Correct Answer: B

QUESTION 10

Universal Containers has created the custom objects Candidate and Interview in Salesforce to track candidates and interviews respectively. The company wants to track the total number of interviews a candidate has gone through on the candidate record without writing any code.

Which two actions should an app builder take to accomplish this requirement? (Choose two.)

A. Use a formula field on the Candidate record to show the total number of interviews.
B. Use a roll-up summary field on the Candidate record to show the total number of interviews.
C. Use a master-detail relationship between the Candidate and Interview objects.
D. Use a lookup relationship between the Candidate and Interview objects.

Correct Answer: BC

QUESTION 11

Universal Containers has deployed custom tabs to Production via change

sets, without including the profile settings. What statement is true about the

visibility of custom tabs in Enterprise Edition?

A. Custom tabs are not deployed.
B. Custom tabs are default on for all users.
C. Custom tabs are not hidden for all users.
D. Custom tabs are default off for all users.

Correct Answer: D

QUESTION 12

Which two report formats can be used as a source report to configure a reporting snapshot? (Choose two.)

A. Summary format
B. Joined format
C. Matrix format
D. Tabular format

Correct Answer: AD

QUESTION 13

In Salesforce Classic, Universal Containers provides access to Salesforce for their Customer Support and Sales Operations teams. Management wants to ensure that when users log in, their home tab provides access to links and documentation that are specifically relevant to their team's function.

How can this requirement be met?

A. Create three home page custom components and three layouts; assign users by team.
B. Create three home page custom components and three layouts; assign user by profile.
C. Create two home page custom components and two layouts; assign to users by team.
D. Create two home page custom components and two layouts; assign to users by profile.

Correct Answer: D

QUESTION 14
Which two should be considered when creating unmanaged packages? (Choose two.)

A. Deploying from a Developer Edition environment.
B. Publishing an application for sale on the AppExchange.
C. Distributing upgradeable components to other Salesforce orgs.
D. Distributing open-source projects on the AppExchange.

Correct Answer: AC

QUESTION 15
Universal Containers would like to optimize routes for its traveling service

personnel. What is the recommended solution to meet this requirement?

A. Configure routing options in a custom object.
B. Configure Territory Hierarchy and rules for route based on Territory.
C. Use geolocation fields with the DISTANCE and GEOLOCATION formulas.
D. Use an AppExchange partner product.

Correct Answer: D

QUESTION 16
Universal Containers is setting up Salesforce for the first time. Management wants the sales and marketing teams to have different navigation menus in the Salesforce Mobile App.

What option is available to an app builder to satisfy this requirement?

A. Create sales and marketing profiles and ensure read access to different objects.
B. Create mobile navigation menus for both the sales and marketing profiles.
C. Create public groups for sales and marketing and create mobile navigation menus for each group.
D. Create roles for sales and marketing and assign a custom homepage layout for each role.

Correct Answer: A

QUESTION 17
An app builder wants to show Groups as the last navigation menu item in the Salesforce Mobile App. However, the app builder is not able to select Groups as one of the items on the drop-down menu.

What could cause this?

A. Groups is showing up in the recent section and not in the navigation menu.
B. Groups cannot be the last item in the navigation menu.
C. Groups is included in the Smart Search items but not on the navigation menu.
D. Groups is not included in the selected list for the navigation menu.

Correct Answer: D

QUESTION 18
Universal Containers wants to automate a business process using workflow. They are aware that workflow rules may cause recursive behavior, and as a result certain actions will only cause workflow rules that didn't fire previously to be retriggered.

What workflow action might cause this behavior? (Choose two.)

A. Workflow Field updates with the "Re-evaluate Workflow Rules After Field Change" field selected.
B. Workflow Tasks where the "Due Date" field is set to "Rule Trigger Date" minus X Days.
C. Workflow Outbound Messages with the "Protected Component" field selected.
D. Workflow E-mails containing hard-coded links with Salesforce IDs referencing specific workflow rules.

Correct Answer: AB

QUESTION 19
A new custom object called Invoices needs to have an invoice date for the date and time it was invoiced.

What field type should be selected for this?

A. Date/Time
B. Time
C. Date/Timestamp
D. Date

Correct Answer: A

QUESTION 20
The VP of Sales at Universal Containers wants to have a set of screens to

guide the inside sales team through collecting and updating data for leads.

How can the app builder accomplish this?

A. Workflow
B. Process Builder
C. Lightning Connect
D. Flow

Correct Answer: D

QUESTION 21
The Director of Marketing has asked the app builder to create a formula field that tracks how many days have elapsed since a contact was sent a marketing communication. The director is only interested in whole units.

What function should be used to return today's date for calculating the difference?

A. DATE()
B. NOW()
C. TODAY()
D. DATEVALUE()

Correct Answer: C

QUESTION 22
Which of the following are types of developer sandboxes environment types in Salesforce? (Choose four.)

A. Developer
B. Developer Pro
C. Partial Copy
D. Full Sandbox
E. Partial Sandbox
F. Full Copy

Correct Answer: ABCD

QUESTION 23
Universal Containers requires e-mails to be sent to additional recipients

when a workflow e-mail alert is triggered from the case object. Which two

field types need to be added to the case object to allow additional recipients on the e-mail alert? (Choose two.)

A. Text field
B. E-mail field
C. Lookup field
D. Formula field

Correct Answer: BC
Section: (none)

Explanation :

QUESTION 24
Which two relationship types can be defined with external objects?
(Choose two.)

A. Cross-Organization Lookup
B. External Lookup
C. Indirect Lookup
D. External Master-Detail

Correct Answer: BC

QUESTION 25
Which two are capabilities of Schema Builder? (Choose two.)

A. Viewing page layouts in a new window.
B. Editing custom settings.
C. Showing selected objects on a page.
D. Creating a new record type.

Correct Answer: AC

QUESTION 26
What is a feature that can extend record access beyond the organization-wide defaults? (Choose two.)

A. Criteria-based sharing rules.

B. Owner-based sharing rules.

C. Public or private groups.

D. Dynamic role hierarchy.

Correct Answer: AB

QUESTION 27

Universal Containers needs to send an Outbound Message to an external

system when a record has been updated. What is the recommended

feature to meet this requirement?

A. Lightning Connect

B. Workflow

C. Process Builder

D. Flow Launcher

Correct Answer: B

QUESTION 28

Universal Containers wants to display a message when an opportunity close date is less than 60 days in the future.

What can be used to display different text on the opportunity record depending on the number of days until the target close date?

A. Workflow Update

B. Process Builder

C. Sales Process

D. Formula Field

Correct Answer: D

QUESTION 29

Which three are true about converting a tabular, summary, or matrix report to a joined report? (Choose three.)

A. Cross filters are not supported in joined reports.

B. The Rows to Display filter is not supported in joined reports.

C. Joined report blocks are formatted as matrix reports.

D. Report formula fields are not supported in joined reports.
E. Bucket fields are not supported in joined reports.

Correct Answer: ABE

QUESTION 30

Universal Containers has deployed custom tabs to Production via change

sets, without including the profile settings or permission sets. What is the

setting for the visibility of custom tabs?

A. Custom tabs are hidden for all users.
B. Custom tabs are default off for all users.
C. Custom tabs are default on for all users.
D. Custom tabs are not deployed.

Correct Answer: A

QUESTION 31

Representatives at Universal Containers uses Salesforce to record
information for new Leads. When new prospects are added, an outbound
message is sent to SAP with the Lead's information.

What automation process will accomplish this without writing any code?

A. Design an Approval Process that sends an outbound message upon
   approval.
B. Create a process using Process Builder to send the outbound
   message.
C. Use Flow to create a wizard that will send an outbound message.
D. Create a Workflow Rule with an outbound message as the action.

Correct Answer: D

QUESTION 32

Users at Universal Containers need to be able to quickly create a

Resource record from the Project record's Chatter feed. How should the

app builder define this functionality?

A. By creating a custom "Detail Page" Button on the Project.
B. By creating a custom "Detail Page" Button on the Resource.
C. By creating a custom "Create a Record" Action on the Project.
D. By creating a custom "Create a Record" Action on the Resource.

Correct Answer: D

QUESTION 33
A sales manager would like to look at an Account record and view charts of

all the related open opportunities, closed/won opportunities, and open

cases. How many report charts can be added to the Account page layout

to meet this requirement?

A. 3
B. 4
C. 2
D. 1

Correct Answer: C

QUESTION 34
Which three field types can be referenced by a Roll-Up Summary field
using SUM? (Choose three.)

A. Number
B. Formula
C. Date
D. Percent
E. Currency

Correct Answer: ADE

QUESTION 35
When an opportunity close date is delayed by more than 60 days, the

manager and the VP of Sales must approve the change. Which two solutions will meet the requirement? (Choose two.)

A. Build an approval process that requires unanimous approval from the manager and VP of Sales.
B. Build a validation rule that does not allow a user to save the opportunity record.
C. Create a workflow rule that checks for close date less than 60 days and add an e-mail alert.
D. Create a Process Builder flow that submits the record for an approval process.

Correct Answer: AD

QUESTION 36
Universal Containers wants to streamline its data capture process by linking fields together. UC wants to do this so that the available values on dependent fields are driven by values selected on controlling fields.

Which three considerations support the stated requirements? (Choose three.)

A. Multi-select picklists can be dependent picklists but not controlling fields.
B. Checkbox fields can be controlling fields but not dependent fields.
C. Standard and custom picklist fields can be dependent fields.
D. Custom picklist fields can be either controlling or dependent fields.
E. The data import wizards only allow values to be imported into a dependent picklist if they match the appropriate controlling field.

Correct Answer: ABD

QUESTION 37
Universal Containers has a junction object called Billings with a primary Master-Detail relationship with Accounts and a secondary Master-Detail relationship with Orders. The app builder has a requirement to change the primary Master-Detail relationship to a Lookup.

What happens to the secondary Master-Detail relationship with Orders?

A. The secondary Master-Detail object relationship needs to be reestablished.
B. The secondary Master-Detail object also converts to a lookup.
C. The secondary Master-Detail object becomes the primary.
D. The secondary Master-Detail object relationship is no longer valid.

Correct Answer: C
Section: (none)

Explanation :

QUESTION 38
Which two statements are true when a new full sandbox is created? (Choose two.)

A. Chatter data will be copied to the sandbox by default.
B. Default e-mail deliverability is set to system e-mail only.
C. Usernames will be modified uniquely for that sandbox.
D. Users' e-mail addresses will not be modified.

Correct Answer: BC

QUESTION 39
When is it recommended to refresh a Full sandbox?

A. Whenever a new Production user is added.
B. Within 3 hours of when it is needed.
C. After a major Production release.
D. After UAT sign-off.

Correct Answer: C

QUESTION 40
What is a true statement in regards to creating custom report types?

A. The detail object in a Master-Detail relationship cannot be added as a secondary object on a custom report type.

B. Any object can be chosen unless the object is not visible to the person creating the report type through security settings.
C. When the primary object is a custom object and is deleted, then the report type and any reports created from it must be deleted manually.
D. Once a report type is saved with a standard or custom primary object, the primary object cannot be changed for that report type.

Correct Answer: D

QUESTION 41
In Salesforce Classic, which three use cases can be accomplished using a custom link? (Choose three.)

A. Navigate to a create a record page with fields pre-populated.
B. Navigate to an Apex Trigger to update the current record.
C. Navigate to a process to update the current record.
D. Navigate to a custom Visual Flow to update the current record.
E. Navigate to an external system using data in Salesforce.

Correct Answer: ACE

QUESTION 42
An app builder needs to change the data types of a few custom fields. The app builder is not able to delete and recreate any of the fields, nor modify any Apex code.

What data type change will require the app builder to perform additional steps in order to retain existing functionality?

A. Changing the data type of a field used in lead conversion from number to text.
B. Changing the data type of a field used as an External ID from number to text.
C. Changing the data type of a field used in an Apex class from number to text.
D. Changing the data type of a field used in a report from text to an encrypted field.

Correct Answer: B

QUESTION 43
A customer service representative at a call center would like to be able to

collect information from customers using a series of question prompts.

What could be used to accomplish this?

A. Workflow Rules
B. Salesforce Connect
C. Flow
D. Process Builder

Correct Answer: C

QUESTION 44

An app builder has been asked to provide users a way to identify a Contact's "Preferred Contact Method" directly on the Contact record. Users need to be able to identify whether a phone number or an e-mail is the Contact's preferred communication method.

What field type will allow the app builder to accomplish this with the fewest fields possible?

A. Picklist
B. E-mail
C. Checkboxes
D. Formula

Correct Answer: A

QUESTION 45

Universal Containers uses a private sharing model for opportunities. This model cannot be changed due to a regional structure. A new sales operations team has been created. This team needs to perform analysis on Opportunity data, and should have read and write access to all Opportunities.

Which two are recommended solutions for the app builder to give the users appropriate access? (Choose two.)

A. Add a manual share for all opportunities with each user on the sales operations team.
B. Create a criteria-based sharing rule to share all opportunities with the sales operations private group.
C. Create a criteria-based sharing rule to share all opportunities with the sales operations public group.
D. Add a permission set with "View All" and "Modify All" opportunity permissions enabled.

Correct Answer: BC

QUESTION 46
Universal Containers has a requirement that an Opportunity should have a field showing the value of its associated account's billing state. This value should not change after the Opportunity has been created.

What is the recommended solution to configure this automation behavior?

A. Formula field
B. Apex
C. Roll-up summary field
D. Workflow

Correct Answer: D

QUESTION 47
Universal Containers conducts evaluations of its sales reps using a custom object consisting of numerical scores and executive comments. The company wants to ensure that only the sales reps, their managers, and their manager's executives can view the rep's evaluation record, but the reps should not be able to view the

executive comment fields on their review. How can these requirements be met?

A. Use a private sharing model granting record access using hierarchy; manage field access with record types and field-level security.
B. Use a private sharing model granting record access using custom settings; manage field access with page layouts and field-level security.
C. Use a private sharing model granting record access using hierarchy; manage field access with field-level security.
D. Use a private sharing model granting record access using custom settings; manage field access with record types and page layouts.

Correct Answer: C

QUESTION 48
Which two statements are true about field update actions from workflow rules and approval processes? (Choose two.)

A. Field updates are tracked in the History related list of a record regardless of whether or not history tracking is set for those fields.
B. Field updates to records based on workflow rules and approval processes do not trigger Validation Rules.
C. Field updates are not available on currency fields if the organization uses multi-currency.
D. Field updates with "Re-evaluate Workflow Rules" selected can cause a recursive loop if the update field is included in a workflow.

Correct Answer: CD

QUESTION 49
Which two objects can be members of a Campaign? (Choose two.)

A. Opportunity
B. Account

C. Lead

D. Contact

Correct Answer: CD

QUESTION 50

At Universal Containers, the VP of Service has requested a visual indicator flag on each case, based on the case priority. High-priority case should be flagged red, medium-priority should be flagged yellow, and low-priority cases should be flagged green.

Which two formulas will accomplish this requirement? (Choose two.)

A. IMAGE(CASE(Priority, "Low", "/img/samples/flag_green.gif", "Medium", "/img/samples/flag_yellow.gif", "High", "img/samples/flag_red.gif", "/s.gif"), "Priority Flag")

B. IF(ISPICKVAL(Priority, "Low"), "/img/samples/flag_green.gif , IF(ISPICKVAL(Priority, "Medium"), "/img/samples/flag_yellow.gif", IF(ISPICKVAL(Priority, "High"), "/img/samples/flag_red.gif, "/s.gif")))

C. CASE(Priority, "Low", "/img/samples/flag_green.gif", "Medium", "/img/samples/flag_yellow.gif", "High", "/img/samples/flag_red.gif", "/s.gif")

D. IMAGE(IF(ISPICKVAL(Priority, "Low"), "/img/samples/flag_green.gif", IF(ISPICKVAL(Priority, "Medium"), "/img/samples/flag_yellow.gif", IF(ISPICKVAL(Priority, "High"), "/img/samples/flag_red.gif", "/s.gif))), "Priority Flag")

Correct Answer: AD

QUESTION 51

The Director of Customer Services wants to know when agents are overwhelmed with high-priority items in the support queue. The Director wants to receive a notification when a new case is open with the status of "New" for more than four business hours.

Which two automation processes should be used to accomplish this? (Choose two.)

A. Flow Builder
B. Process Builder
C. Escalation rules
D. Scheduled Apex

Correct Answer: BC

QUESTION 52
Which three statements are true about converting a Lead? (Choose three.)

A. The system automatically maps standard lead fields to standard account, contact, and opportunity fields.
B. Administrators may choose whether to enforce validation rules and triggers.
C. Multi-select picklist values on Lead records overwrite values on Contact's corresponding field.
D. Users can convert leads that are associated with an active approval process.
E. The Lead's most recent campaign record is automatically applied to the "Primary Campaign Source" field on the opportunity.

Correct Answer: ABE

QUESTION 53
The organization-wide default for a custom object is set to private. The Supervisor profile grants view access to the same object. A user with the Supervisor profile is also listed as the Manager on the user detail records for a subordinate. However, the Supervisor still cannot view records owned

by the subordinate.

Which two issues are preventing the Supervisor from viewing records owned by the subordinate? (Choose two.)

A. Organization-wide settings for the custom object grant access to other users with the same role.
B. The Supervisor requires a permission set in order to view the subordinate's records.
C. The Supervisor's role is not above the subordinate's role in the hierarchy.
D. Organization-wide settings for the custom object do not grant access using hierarchy.

Correct Answer: CD

QUESTION 54

A custom object named Assignment has private sharing setting that grants access using hierarchies. The organization has a role hierarchy where each Territory Manager reports to an Area Manager, who reports to a VP of Sales. The VP of Sales is at the top of the role hierarchy. A user who is in the Area Manager role creates a new Assignment record.

Who can see this record?

A. The record owner only.
B. The record owner and the VP of Sales.
C. The record owner and all of the other Area Managers.
D. The record owner and all of the Territory Managers in their hierarchy.

Correct Answer: B

QUESTION 55

The app builder at Universal Containers has been asked to ensure that when an Opportunity record exceeding $20k is being saved, details have been captured in the Comments field.

What can be used to meet this requirement?

A. Process Builder
B. Validation Rule
C. Approval Process
D. Workflow

Correct Answer: B

QUESTION 56
The VP of Marketing wants to broadcast an e-mail to 10,000 contacts in Salesforce on a regular basis, but realizes Salesforce's mass e-mail functionality has a

limitation on the number of e-mails that can be sent each day. What action

should the app builder take?

A. Request Salesforce increase the number of maximum daily e-mails.
B. Download all Contacts to a CSV file and use an e-mail client to send the e-mails.
C. Develop Apex code and Visualforce pages to send the e-mails.
D. Research and evaluate products available on AppExchange to send mass e-mails.

Correct Answer: D

QUESTION 57
An app builder is loading data into Salesforce. To link new records back to the legacy system, a field will be used to track the legacy ID on the Account object. For future data loads this ID will be used when upserting records.

Which two fields attributes should be selected? (Choose two.)

A. External ID
B. Text (encrypted)
C. Required
D. Unique

Correct Answer: AD

QUESTION 58
Which two are features of Schema Builder? (Choose two.)

A. To create new relationships on standard and custom objects.
B. To create a Geolocation custom field on custom objects.

C. To view and edit c

D. ustom field level permissions.
E. To modify properties on standard and custom objects.

Correct Answer: AD

QUESTION 59
Launch a troubleshooting wizard from a button, at the end of which a

knowledge article is created if it'd be helpful to other users. Which tool

would you use for the following use case?

A. Process builder
B. Flow
C. Workflow
D. Approvals

Correct Answer: B

QUESTION 60
When an opportunity has a discount of more than 40%, notify the CEO via

e-mail and request sign-off. Provide a way for the CEO to leave comments.

Which tool would you use for the following use case?

A. Process builder
B. Flow
C. Workflow
D. Approvals

Correct Answer: D
Section: (none)

Explanation :

QUESTION 61
When an opportunity closes, close all activities related to that opportunity

automatically and create a renewal opportunity. Which tool would you use

for the following use case?

A. Process builder
B. Flow
C. Workflow
D. Approvals

Correct Answer: A

QUESTION 62
As an account's expiration approaches, send recurring e-mail notifications

to the owner (2 weeks before, 1 week before, 3 days before, and 1 day

before). Which tool would you use for the following use case?

A. Process builder
B. Flow
C. Workflow
D. Approvals

Correct Answer: C

QUESTION 63

You can configure access to data at all of the following levels, except.

A. Organization
B. Objects
C. Page layouts
D. Records

Correct Answer: C

QUESTION 64
You can secure data at the organization level, using all of these methods, except.

A. Limit Login IP addresses
B. Limit Login Hours
C. Set password policies
D. Use hardware token

Correct Answer: D

QUESTION 65
Which of these is not a method for controlling record-level access?

A. Organization-Wide Defaults
B. Role Hierarchy
C. Profiles
D. Sharing Rules

Correct Answer: C

QUESTION 66
How can you control object level access? (Choose two.)

A. Profiles

B. Permission Sets
C. Roles
D. Groups
E. OWD

Correct Answer: AB

QUESTION 67
Where can a Standard Lightning Component be placed in the Lightning app builder tool?

A. Canvas
B. Console Layout
C. Mini Page Layout
D. Mobile Card

Correct Answer: A

QUESTION 68
Universal Container's app builder needs to display an account's rating on all contacts related to that account.

Which formula is valid in a text formula field on the contact to display the appropriate value? (Choose two.)

A. CASE(Account.Rating, Hot, Hot, Warm, Warm, Cold, Cold, Not Rated)
B. CASE(Account.Rating, "Hot", "Hot", "Warm", "Warm", "Cold", "Cold", "Not Rated")
C. Account.Rating
D. Text(Account.Rating)

Correct Answer: BD

QUESTION 69
Universal Containers has limited in-house development resources, but would like to support online payment processing for its products.

What is the recommended solution to meet this requirement?

A. Configure price books, products, and payment schedules to enable this capability.
B. Work with developers to develop custom code for payment processing.
C. Configure Outbound Messaging to send a message to an external Payment Gateway.
D. Install an AppExchange product to provide Payment Gateway processing.

Correct Answer: D

QUESTION 70

All of the following are advantages of the Schema Builder except.

A. All object and field relationship details are available from one screen.
B. You can view fields and relationships for custom, but not standard objects.
C. Schema Builder shows details like field values, required fields, and how objects are related.
D. It's easy to build objects and fields directly from the Schema Builder, allowing you to visualize and change relationships with ease.

Correct Answer: B

QUESTION 71

What should be done to create a custom object from the Schema Builder?

A. From the Objects tab, select New>Object.
B. From the Elements tab, drag Object onto the canvas.
C. Right-click in the canvas and select "New Object".

Correct Answer: B

QUESTION 72

What should be done to create a custom field from the Schema Builder?

A. From the Objects tab, select New>Field.
B. From the Elements tab, drag a field type onto the canvas.

C. In the canvas, right-click an object and select "New Field".

Correct Answer: B

QUESTION 73
To leverage flows you need to.

A. Have Run Flows permission enabled.
B. Have access to the Visualforce page the flow uses.
C. The flow must be active.
D. All of the above.

Correct Answer: D

QUESTION 74
Which three statements are true about Master-Detail relationships?
(Choose three.)

A. You can't convert it if there is a roll-up summary field.
B. Converting a look-up to master detail changes the OWD to Controlled by Parent.
C. A look-up can be converted to a master detail if there are existing records with null values.
D. SF displays a waiting page after you request to change a master detail to a look-up or vice versa.

Correct Answer: ABD

QUESTION 75
What happens when you convert a picklist to a multi-select picklist?
(Choose two.)

A. Values are retained.

B. Values not in the picklist are deleted from existing records when the data type changes.
C. Data is lost.
D. You can't convert to a multi-select picklist.

Correct Answer: AB

QUESTION 76
If data is lost, any list view based on the custom field will be deleted, and assignment and escalation rules may be affected.

A. True
B. False

Correct Answer: A

QUESTION 77
You can convert a Text Area(Long) to E-mail, Phone, Text, Text Area or URL without data loss.

A. True
B. False

Correct Answer: A

QUESTION 78
You cannot change auto number to text and vice versa and not lose your data.

A. True

B. False

Correct Answer: B

QUESTION 79
You can have multiple records with the same external ID.

A. True

B. False

Correct Answer: A

Explanation: It is not recommended, as it will defeat the purpose of the external id.

QUESTION 80

What is true about a master detail relationship? (Choose three.)

A. To create multilevel master-detail relationships, you need the "Customize Application" user permission.
B. Standard objects can't be on the detail side of a custom object in a master-detail relationship.
C. You can create a master-detail relationship if the custom object already contains data.
D. You can create a relationship as a lookup and then convert it to master-detail if the lookup field in all records contains a value.
E. By default, records can be reparented master-detail relationships.

Correct Answer: ABD

QUESTION 81

What is true about Junction objects?

A. Junction object records are deleted when either associated master record is deleted and placed in the Recycle Bin.
B. If both associated master records are deleted, the junction object record is deleted permanently and can't be restored.
C. The first master-detail relationship you create on your junction object becomes the primary relationship.
D. All of the above.

Correct Answer: D

QUESTION 82

What type of relationships can you create on External Objects? (Choose all that apply.)

A. Lookup
B. External lookup
C. Indirect lookup
D. Direct lookup
E. All of the above

Correct Answer: ABC

QUESTION 83
Indirect lookup relationship fields can be created on external objects only.

A. True
B. False

Correct Answer: A

QUESTION 84
What is true about external lookup relationship fields? (Choose all that apply.)

A. Lookup filters are available for external lookup relationship fields.
B. Cascade-delete isn't available for external object relationships.
C. Only objects that have a custom field with the External ID and Unique attributes are available as parent objects in indirect lookup relationships.
D. All of the above.

Correct Answer: BC

QUESTION 85
Each workflow rule applies to a single object.

A. True

B. False

Correct Answer: A

QUESTION 86

Workflow rules on custom objects are NOT automatically deleted if the custom object is deleted.

A. True

B. False

Correct Answer: B

QUESTION 87

What are use cases for Validation Rules?

A. Enforce conditionally required fields

B. Enforce proper data format

C. Enforce consistency

D. Prevent data loss

E. All of the above

Correct Answer: E

QUESTION 88

What are the steps for creating a dynamic approval process?

A. Create (user) lookup fields on the object being approved, Create a custom object as an approval matrix, Populate the approval matrix record, Create Apex code to populate the user fields from the approval matrix record, Create or update an approval process to utilize the new lookup fields.

B. Create standard object as an approval matrix.

C. Create an approval process.

D. All of the above.

Correct Answer: A

QUESTION 89

For an external object relationship, you can create an indirect lookup relationship. What type of object(s) can be the parent?

A. External
B. Standard or Custom
C. Standard or External
D. Custom

Correct Answer: B

Explanation: For an indirect lookup you can have standard or custom objects as the parent, but can only have an external object as the child. Does not require a Salesforce ID.

QUESTION 90
A Lightning component is a compact, configurable, and reusable element that you can drag and drop onto a Lightning Page in the Lightning app builder.

A. True
B. False

Correct Answer: A

QUESTION 91
What are the standard Lightning components?

A. Filter List
B. Recent Items
C. Report Chart
D. Rich Text
E. Visualforce Page
F. All of the above

Correct Answer: F

QUESTION 92
What can you build with the Lightning app builder?

A. At-a-glance, dashboard-style apps.

B. Apps optimized for a particular task.
C. Simple, single-page apps with drill-down capability.
D. All of the above.

Correct Answer: D

QUESTION 93
Actions on a Lightning Page allow you to.

A. Send e-mail, create a task, and create or update records.
B. Send e-mail and delete or clone records.
C. Clone records, add users, and assign permissions.
D. Send e-mail, send outbound messages, and launch a flow.

Correct Answer: A

QUESTION 94

Use the data import wizard when. (Choose three.)

A. You need to load less than 50,000 records.
B. The objects you need to import are supported by the wizard.
C. You want to schedule regular data loads, such as nightly imports.
D. You don't need the import process to be automate.

Correct Answer: ABD

QUESTION 95
Use Data Loader when. (Choose three.)

A. You need to load 50,000 to five million records. If you need to load more than 5 million records, we recommend you work with a Salesforce partner or visit the AppExchange for a suitable partner product.

B. You don't need the import process to be automated.
C. You need to load into an object that is not supported by the Data Import Wizard.
D. You want to schedule regular data loads, such as nightly imports.

Correct Answer: ACD

QUESTION 96
You can export data from Salesforce using any of the following methods except.

A. Use the data Manager tool to manually request an export of all the data in your organization.
B. Use the data Export wizard within SF to export data manually or automatically.
C. Use the data loader client application.
D. Log a case with SF.

Correct Answer: A

QUESTION 97
When using the Data Export Wizard to manually export data, you can only export data if.

A. Your data doesn't include attachments, images, or documents.
B. You've installed a client application to export the data.
C. Enough time has passed since your last export.
D. You are an Admin.

Correct Answer: C

QUESTION 98
When scheduling automatic data exporting with the Data Export Wizard, you must specify all of the following except.

A. Start and end dates
B. Time of day
C. Number of attachments
D. Frequency, if your organization supports monthly exports

Correct Answer: C

QUESTION 99
Recursive triggers may cause your organization to exceed its limit for workflow time triggers per hour.

A. True
B. False

Correct Answer: A

QUESTION 100
When do you need to refresh a sandbox? (Choose two.)

A. 3 Hours before you need it.
B. When modification have been made to the production organization.
C. Anytime.
D. When you are done making changes to it.

Correct Answer: BD

QUESTION 101
Which of the following can you create safely in a production organization?

A. Apex Classes
B. Triggers
C. Custom Apex Controllers for Visualforce Pages
D. Reports and dashboards

Correct Answer: D

QUESTION 102
Which of the following are good ways to track changes in production?

A. Diff the metadata.
B. Use a change log request form.
C. Check the setup audit trail every week.
D. All of the above.

Correct Answer: D

QUESTION 103
You've developed some new functionality in production, but there are

concurrent development projects in a developer sandbox. What's the best

way to make sure the changes in production and projects in development

are both merged?

A. Simply refresh the developer sandbox.
B. Copy all of the sandbox metadata to a file system, then refresh the
    developer sandbox, and finally deploy all the metadata to the developer
    sandbox.
C. Create a new sandbox, and then deploy from your developer sandbox
    to the new sandbox.
D. None of the above.

Correct Answer: C

QUESTION 104
You have a requirement to ensure that if the discount field on an opp is

greater than 30%, the record should be automatically submitted for

Approval. Which of the following would help you meet this requirement?

(Choose two.)

A. Approval Process
B. Workflow
C. Process Builder
D. Visual Workflow

Correct Answer: CD

QUESTION 105

What is not true regarding relating Tasks and Events to other objects?

A. Accounts are associated via the WhatID or AccountID.
B. Leads are associated via the WhoID.
C. Custom Objects are associated via the What ID.
D. Assets are associated via the WhatID.
E. Contacts are associated via the WhatID.

Correct Answer: E

Explanation: Contacts are associated via the WhatID.

QUESTION 106
What is true regarding changing the field type of a rich text area?

A. It is not possible to change the field type of a rich text area.
B. Rich text area fields can be converted but only to a long text area field type.
C. Images in a rich text area are deleted when the field type is converted.
D. Rich text area fields can be converted to a text area field type but data may be truncate.

Correct Answer: B

QUESTION 107
Universal Containers provides access to Salesforce for their sales, service and marketing teams. Management wants to ensure that when users log in, their home tab provides access to links and documentation that are specifically relevant to their job function.

How can this requirement be met?
A. Create separate home page custom components and layouts; assign to users by role.
B. Create separate home page custom components and layouts; assign to users by profile.
C. Expose specific elements within a home page custom component determined by role.
D. Expose specific elements within a home page custom components determined by profile.

Correct Answer: B

QUESTION 108

Which capability allows an app builder to grant object-level access? (Choose two.)

A. Assigning a user a Profile that allows Read access to an object.
B. Assigning a user a Public Group that allows for Read and Edit access to an object.
C. Assigning a user a Permission Set that allows Read and Edit access to an object.
D. Assigning a user a Role that allows Read access to an object.

Correct Answer: AC

QUESTION 109
Universal containers would like to use a chatter group for their mergers and acquisition team to collaborate on potential new projects. This group should not be visible for non-members to see or join, and can be accessed by invite only.

Which chatter Group type should the app builder recommend?

A. Member Group
B. Unlisted Group
C. Public Group
D. Private Group

Correct Answer: B

QUESTION 110
An app builder has been asked to integrate Salesforce with an external

web service. The web service must be notified every time an opportunity is

won. What are two ways to satisfy this requirement? (Choose two.)

A. Use flow with outbound message.
B. Use a process and apex code.
C. Use a process and an outbound message.
D. Use workflow with an outbound message.

Correct Answer: BD

QUESTION 111
An app builder wants to prevent users from creating new records on an

account related list by overriding standard buttons. Which two aspects

should be considered before overriding standard buttons? (Choose two.)

A. Standard buttons that are NOT available for overrides can still be hidden
   on page layouts.
B. Standard buttons can be changed on lookup dialogs, list views, and
   search result layouts.
C. Standard buttons can be overridden, relocated on the detail page, and
   relabeled.
D. Standard button can be overridden with a VF page.

Correct Answer: AD

Explanation:
If a button isn't available for overrides, you can still hide it on the page
layout.
For each experience—Salesforce Classic, Lightning Experience, or
mobile—click the type of override you want associated with the action
Visualforce page—Use the behavior from a Visualforce page.

References:
https://help.salesforce.com/articleView?id=links_override_considerations.ht
m&type=5
https://help.salesforce.com/articleView?id=links_customize_override.htm&t
ype=5

QUESTION 112
Universal Containers uses a custom object to track expense reports. They

would like to automatically post updates on a record's feed whenever an expense report has been approved.

What social feature can be used to accomplish this?

A. Approval process
B. Feed Quick Action
C. Auto-response rule
D. Feed tracking

Correct Answer: D

QUESTION 113
The CRM Manager at Universal Containers has requested that a custom

text field be converted to a picklist in order to promote better data hygiene.

Which two actions should be considered before changing the field type?

(Choose two.)

A. Changing a field type will remove existing field history.
B. Field reference will be removed in Visualforce pages.
C. Existing list views that reference the field may be deleted.
D. All data should be backed up before converting a text field.

Correct Answer: CD

QUESTION 114
What of the following are general types of actions available in Salesforce?
(Choose four.)

A. Update – Update Records
B. Create – create a record
C. Log a Call – log a call and it is recorded as a task
D. Custom – requires visual force page
E. Remove – Remove a record
F. Delete – permanently remove a record

Correct Answer: ABCD

QUESTION 115
Which of the following are types of developer sandboxes environment types in Salesforce? (Choose four.)

A. Developer
B. Developer Pro
C. Partial Copy
D. Full Sandbox
E. Partial Sandbox
F. Full Copy

Correct Answer: ABCD

QUESTION 116
Which of the following statements are true about Record IDs? (Choose two.)

A. The 18 character ID is case?insensitive
B. The 15 character ID is case?insensitive
C. The 18 character ID is case?sensitive
D. The 15 character ID is case?sensitive

Correct Answer: AD

QUESTION 117
What is the maximum number of master-detail lookup relationships allowable per object?

A. 1
B. 2
C. 3
D. 4

Correct Answer: B

QUESTION 118

Which three options are available for assigning access to Lightning Pages using Lightning App Builder? (Choose three.)

A. Profile and permission sets
B. App default
C. Role and subordinates
D. The org default
E. App, record type, profile

Correct Answer: BDE

QUESTION 119
What language is used to query Salesforce for specific information?

A. Apex
B. SOQL
C. SQL
D. SOSL

Correct Answer: B

QUESTION 120
Which two of the following are supported actions for the Global Actions Menu? (Choose two.)

A. Launch a custom Canvas App
B. Upload a new Chatter File
C. Post to a Chatter feed
D. Launch a custom Lighting Component

Correct Answer: AD

QUESTION 121
Which type of custom fields can be used as External ID? (Choose three.)

A. Email

B. Date

C. A text field that is unique

D. A text field that is encrypted

E. Phone

F. A text field that is required

Correct Answer: ACF

Explanation:
Encrypted cannot be external ID.

QUESTION 122
Which statements are correct about encrypted fields among the following?
(Choose four.)

A. Encrypted fields can be included in search results, and report results.

B. They are not available for use in filters such as list views, reports, roll-up summary fields, and rule filters.

C. Encrypted text fields can be an external ID and can have default values.

D. Encrypted fields are not available in lead conversion, workflow rule criteria or formulas, formula fields, outbound messages, default values, and Web-to-Lead and Web-to-Case forms.

E. Encrypted fields are not searchable and cannot be used to define report criteria.

Correct Answer: ABDE

QUESTION 123
What is not a possible action of the Lightning Process Builder?

A. Trigger APEX

B. Update a record

C. Trigger a Flow

D. Send an Outbound message

Correct Answer: D

QUESTION 124
Which of these is true about the Lookup Relationship?

A. Security access of the child record is dependent upon the parent record.
B. Deleting an object deletes its children.
C. Roll-up Summary Field can be used to perform basic operations over all children of a parent record.
D. Parent is not a required field and may be omitted.

Correct Answer: D

QUESTION 125
Which of these is not a valid report type?

A. Detailed
B. Summary
C. Matrix
D. Tabular

Correct Answer: A

QUESTION 126
When changing a fields data type, which scenario can you expect data loss? (Choose two.)

A. Number to Text
B. Text to Picklist
C. Currency to Number
D. Email to Text

Correct Answer: AB

QUESTION 127
Which Action Type is not available when working with Global Actions?

A. Create a Record
B. Update a Record
C. Log a Call
D. Custom Visualforce

Correct Answer: B

QUESTION 128
What is true about a junction object?

A. A standard object that has two Master-Detail relationships.
B. A standard object that has one Master-Detail relationship.
C. A custom object that has two Master-Detail relationships.
D. A custom object that has one Master-Detail relationship.

Correct Answer: C

QUESTION 129
Which of the following is not a valid return type of a custom formula?

A. Text
B. Array
C. Date
D. Decimal

Correct Answer: B

QUESTION 130
When Record Types control picklist values, you need to. (Choose two.)

A. If removed from picklist, value won't be available on any record types but the value on existing record will not change.

B. You need to manually add values to Opportunity Source, Lead Source and Case source.
C. Manually add values to the Record Types.
D. Other option.

Correct Answer: AC

QUESTION 131
Which statements are true regarding Roll-Up Summary Fields? (Choose three.)

A. Automatically derived fields, such as current date or current user, are allowed in a Roll-up Summary Field.
B. Because Roll-up Summary Fields are not displayed on edit pages, you can use them in validation rules.
C. Once created, you cannot change the detail object selected or delete any field referenced in your Roll-up Summary definition.
D. Validation errors can display when saving either the detail or master record.
E. Advanced currency management has no affect on Roll-up Summary Fields.

Correct Answer: BCD

QUESTION 132
Global actions can be created to let users create which of the following kinds of records? (Choose three.)

A. Question
B. Event (without invitees)
C. Products
D. Opportunity
E. Chatter Post
F. Users

Correct Answer: ABD

QUESTION 133

Which Salesforce Formula Function can return a value based on more than two different field parameters?

A. Contains
B. Case Statement
C. Beings
D. IF Statement

Correct Answer: B

QUESTION 134

An organization wants to create a field to store manager data on the user

object. The manager field is a reference to another user record. What type

of relationship should be used?

A. Master-Detail
B. Lookup
C. Many-to-many
D. Hierarchical

Correct Answer: D

Explanation:
Hierarchical relationship: This type of relationship is a special lookup relationship available only for the user object. It allows users to use a lookup field to associate one user with another that does not directly or indirectly refer to itself. For example, you can create a custom hierarchical relationship field to store each user's direct manager.

QUESTION 135

In terms of the order of execution, what must be taken into account when using Validation rules & Workflows?

A. The order of execution can be controlled in Salesforce setup.
B. Validation rules fire before Workflow rules therefore will not catch any

data that does not abide by your Validation rules.

C. Validation rules fire after Workflow rules, so you must ensure that Workflow rules abide by your Validation rules to avoid errors.

D. Validation rules & Workflow rules fire on separate automation schedules and therefore the order of execution can be ignored.

Correct Answer: B

Explanation:
Salesforce processes any rules in the following order:
1. Validation rules
2. Assignment rules
3. Auto-response rules
4. Workflow rules (with immediate actions)
5. Escalation rules

QUESTION 136
To enable the Publisher Actions area on Page Layouts, navigate to.

A. Setup | Customize | Actions | Settings
B. Setup | Customize | Chatter | Settings
C. Setup | Customize | <Objects> | Settings
D. Setup | Customize | Feeds | Settings

Correct Answer: B

QUESTION 137
In a data model object, A is related to B, B is related to C. How will a

developer create a report to include fields of A & C?

A. Create a custom report with A and C fields as the relationship already exists.

B. Create a custom report type with A, B and C, and use it in the report.
C. Create lookup relationships between A, B and C.
D. Report cannot be created.

Correct Answer: B

QUESTION 138
What determines whether a user can create a new record using a specific record type?

A. Sharing

B. Field level security

C. Page layout

D. Profile

Correct Answer: D

QUESTION 139

Use case:

An object called "House" is related to Opportunity, there can be many Houses per Opportunity. On houses, we have a field named "Square feet". We need to show the total of Square feet for all houses on each Opportunity.

What type of relationship should we have?

A. Cross-Object

B. Master-Detail

C. Lookup

D. Junction

Correct Answer: B

QUESTION 140

Object A has a lookup to object B.

Which of the following statements are true? (Choose two.)

A. Fields of object B can be accessed from object A.

B. Fields of both B and A are accessible from object A.

C. Fields of object A can be accessed from object.

D. Fields of both A and B are accessible from object.

Correct Answer: AB

QUESTION 141

ABC Company has a custom object "Service" which has a lookup relationship to Account. ABC Company wants to enhance Salesforce1 with an action that allows account managers to enter a new service to an

Account while looking at the account.

What should be done?

A. Enter an object specific action to Service and put it in the Account Layout.
B. Enter an object specific action to Service and put it in the Service Layout.
C. Enter an object specific action to Account and put it in the Service Layout.
D. Enter an object specific action to Account and put it in the Account Layout.

Correct Answer: D

Explanation:

On Account, you would create an action with target object of Service, and then put this button on the Account layout.

QUESTION 142
A developer wants to make sure that all fields on his new custom object

are editable to all profiles. What should be checked on field level security?

A. Enable Visible and Read-Only.
B. Enable Visible but Disable Read-Only.
C. Disable Visible but Enable Read-Only.
D. Disable Visible and Read-Only.

Correct Answer: B

QUESTION 143
How can you make a field mandatory? (Choose three.)

A. Create a Workflow Rule.
B. Check the required field box on the page layout.
C. Check the required field box on the field definition.
D. Creating a validation rule for the field.
E. Check the required field box for the field on the record type.

Correct Answer: BCD

Explanation:
Required while creating: Cannot be bypassed by any way (API/Dataloader/Imports).
Required on Page Layout: Required only when one works on the UI (inline editing/creating record on page/edit record on page).

QUESTION 144
ABC Company installs an unmanaged package.

Which of the following are true? (Choose two.)

A. Unmanaged packages have a namespace prefix.
B. Components of unmanaged packages can be edited.
C. Unmanaged packages don't have a version number.
D. Unmanaged packages can be upgraded.
E. Tests are executed during deployment.

Correct Answer: BE

Explanation:
unmanaged cannot be upgraded *unmanaged have a version number* *unmanaged namespace is removed* *all need 75% code coverage during deployment*

QUESTION 145
In a master-detail relationship scenario, the fields of the parent object need

to be displayed in the related list. How will a developer achieve this design?

A. Workflow rule
B. Validation rule
C. Assignment rule
D. Cross-object formula field

Correct Answer: D

Explanation:
Cross-object formulas can reference merge fields from a master ("parent")
object if an object is on the detail side of a master-detail relationship.
Cross-object formulas also work with lookup relationships. You can
reference fields from objects that are up to 10 relationships away.